NAME:

CONTACT:

.

· Today I am grateful for ·

_____

_____

_____

· What would make today great? ·

_____

_____

_____

· Positive affirmations. I am... ·

_____

_____

- →

· Amazing things I experienced today: ·

_____

_____

_____

· What am I looking forward to tomorrow? ·

_____

_____

_____

· Today I am grateful for ·

_____

_____

_____

· What would make today great? ·

_____

_____

_____

· Positive affirmations. I am... ·

_____

_____

_____

- ➤

· Amazing things I experienced today: ·

_____

_____

_____

· What am I looking forward to tomorrow? ·

_____

_____

_____

DATE:

· Today I am grateful for ·

_____

_____

_____

· What would make today great? ·

_____

_____

_____

· Positive affirmations. I am... ·

_____

_____

- ➤

· Amazing things I experienced today: ·

_____

_____

_____

· What am I looking forward to tomorrow? ·

_____

_____

_____

DATE:

☀

· Today I am grateful for ·

_____

_____

_____

· What would make today great? ·

_____

_____

_____

· Positive affirmations. I am... ·

_____

_____

✂ - ➤

🌙

· Amazing things I experienced today: ·

_____

_____

_____

· What am I looking forward to tomorrow? ·

_____

_____

_____

☼

· Today I am grateful for ·

_____

_____

_____

· What would make today great? ·

_____

_____

_____

· Positive affirmations. I am... ·

_____

_____

- ➤

☾

· Amazing things I experienced today: ·

_____

_____

_____

· What am I looking forward to tomorrow? ·

_____

_____

_____

DATE:

☼ · Today I am grateful for ·

_____

_____

_____

· What would make today great? ·

_____

_____

_____

· Positive affirmations. I am... ·

_____

_____

- →

☾ · Amazing things I experienced today: ·

_____

_____

_____

· What am I looking forward to tomorrow? ·

_____

_____

_____

DATE:

☀ · Today I am grateful for ·

_____

_____

_____

· What would make today great? ·

_____

_____

_____

· Positive affirmations. I am... ·

_____

_____

✂ - →

☾ · Amazing things I experienced today: ·

_____

_____

_____

· What am I looking forward to tomorrow? ·

_____

_____

_____

WEEKLY INSPIRATION

> **DON'T JUDGE EACH DAY BY THE HARVEST**
> **THAT YOU REAP**
> **BUT BY THE SEEDS THAT YOU**
> **PLANT.**

—

Robert Louis Stevenson

WRITE YOUR OWN QUOTE:

> "
>
>
> "

· Today I am grateful for ·

· What would make today great? ·

· Positive affirmations. I am... ·

· Amazing things I experienced today: ·

· What am I looking forward to tomorrow? ·

· Today I am grateful for ·

_____

_____

_____

· What would make today great? ·

_____

_____

_____

· Positive affirmations. I am... ·

_____

_____

- ->

· Amazing things I experienced today: ·

_____

_____

_____

· What am I looking forward to tomorrow? ·

_____

_____

_____

· Today I am grateful for ·

_____

_____

_____

· What would make today great? ·

_____

_____

_____

· Positive affirmations. I am... ·

_____

_____

✂ - →

· Amazing things I experienced today: ·

_____

_____

_____

· What am I looking forward to tomorrow? ·

_____

_____

_____

· Today I am grateful for ·

_____

_____

_____

· What would make today great? ·

_____

_____

_____

· Positive affirmations. I am... ·

_____

_____

_____

· Amazing things I experienced today: ·

_____

_____

_____

· What am I looking forward to tomorrow? ·

_____

_____

_____

DATE:

· Today I am grateful for ·

_____

_____

_____

· What would make today great? ·

_____

_____

_____

· Positive affirmations. I am... ·

_____

_____

-->

· Amazing things I experienced today: ·

_____

_____

_____

· What am I looking forward to tomorrow? ·

_____

_____

_____

· Today I am grateful for ·

_____

_____

_____

· What would make today great? ·

_____

_____

_____

· Positive affirmations. I am... ·

_____

_____

_____

· Amazing things I experienced today: ·

_____

_____

_____

· What am I looking forward to tomorrow? ·

_____

_____

_____

· Today I am grateful for ·

_____

_____

_____

· What would make today great? ·

_____

_____

_____

· Positive affirmations. I am... ·

_____

_____

- ▶

· Amazing things I experienced today: ·

_____

_____

_____

· What am I looking forward to tomorrow? ·

_____

_____

_____

WEEKLY INSPIRATION

" WHEN YOU ARISE IN THE MORNING, THINK
OF WHAT A PRECIOUS PRIVILEGE IT IS TO
BE ALIVE – TO BREATHE, TO THINK, TO
ENJOY, TO LOVE. "

—

Marcus Aurelius

WRITE YOUR OWN QUOTE:

"

"

☀

· Today I am grateful for ·

_____

_____

_____

· What would make today great? ·

_____

_____

_____

· Positive affirmations. I am... ·

_____

_____

✂ - ➤

☾

· Amazing things I experienced today: ·

_____

_____

_____

· What am I looking forward to tomorrow? ·

_____

_____

_____

· Today I am grateful for ·

· What would make today great? ·

· Positive affirmations. I am... ·

· Amazing things I experienced today: ·

· What am I looking forward to tomorrow? ·

· Today I am grateful for ·

_____

_____

_____

· What would make today great? ·

_____

_____

_____

· Positive affirmations. I am... ·

_____

_____

- →

· Amazing things I experienced today: ·

_____

_____

_____

· What am I looking forward to tomorrow? ·

_____

_____

_____

· Today I am grateful for ·

_____

_____

_____

· What would make today great? ·

_____

_____

_____

· Positive affirmations. I am... ·

_____

_____

_____

- ➤

· Amazing things I experienced today: ·

_____

_____

_____

· What am I looking forward to tomorrow? ·

_____

_____

_____

- Today I am grateful for -

_____

_____

_____

- What would make today great? -

_____

_____

_____

- Positive affirmations. I am... -

_____

_____

_____

✂ - ➤

- Amazing things I experienced today: -

_____

_____

_____

- What am I looking forward to tomorrow? -

_____

_____

_____

· Today I am grateful for ·

_____

_____

_____

· What would make today great? ·

_____

_____

_____

· Positive affirmations. I am... ·

_____

_____

- →

· Amazing things I experienced today: ·

_____

_____

_____

· What am I looking forward to tomorrow? ·

_____

_____

_____

· Today I am grateful for ·

· What would make today great? ·

· Positive affirmations. I am... ·

- ▶

· Amazing things I experienced today: ·

· What am I looking forward to tomorrow? ·

WEEKLY INSPIRATION

"

IF THE WORLD SEEMS COLD TO YOU,
KINDLE FIRES TO WARM IT

"

—

Lucy Larcom

WRITE YOUR OWN QUOTE:

"

"

☀

· Today I am grateful for ·

_____

_____

_____

· What would make today great? ·

_____

_____

_____

· Positive affirmations. I am... ·

_____

_____

- →

☾

· Amazing things I experienced today: ·

_____

_____

_____

· What am I looking forward to tomorrow? ·

_____

_____

_____

· Today I am grateful for ·

_____

_____

· What would make today great? ·

_____

_____

· Positive affirmations. I am... ·

_____

_____

- ->

· Amazing things I experienced today: ·

_____

_____

· What am I looking forward to tomorrow? ·

_____

_____

_____

· Today I am grateful for ·

_____

_____

_____

· What would make today great? ·

_____

_____

_____

· Positive affirmations. I am... ·

_____

_____

- →

· Amazing things I experienced today: ·

_____

_____

_____

· What am I looking forward to tomorrow? ·

_____

_____

_____

· Today I am grateful for ·

_____

_____

_____

· What would make today great? ·

_____

_____

_____

· Positive affirmations. I am... ·

_____

_____

- →

· Amazing things I experienced today: ·

_____

_____

_____

· What am I looking forward to tomorrow? ·

_____

_____

_____

· Today I am grateful for ·

_____

_____

_____

· What would make today great? ·

_____

_____

_____

· Positive affirmations. I am... ·

_____

_____

- ▶

· Amazing things I experienced today: ·

_____

_____

_____

· What am I looking forward to tomorrow? ·

_____

_____

_____

· Today I am grateful for ·

· What would make today great? ·

· Positive affirmations. I am... ·

· Amazing things I experienced today: ·

· What am I looking forward to tomorrow? ·

· Today I am grateful for ·

_____

_____

_____

· What would make today great? ·

_____

_____

_____

· Positive affirmations. I am... ·

_____

_____

_____

- ➤

· Amazing things I experienced today: ·

_____

_____

_____

· What am I looking forward to tomorrow? ·

_____

_____

_____

_____

WEEKLY INSPIRATION

" USE YOUR HEALTH, EVEN TO THE POINT OF
WEARING IT OUT. THAT IS WHAT IT IS FOR.
SPEND ALL YOU HAVE BEFORE YOU DIE: DO
NOT OUTLIVE YOURSELF. "

–

George Bernard Shaw

WRITE YOUR OWN QUOTE:

"

"

· Today I am grateful for ·

_____

_____

_____

· What would make today great? ·

_____

_____

_____

· Positive affirmations. I am... ·

_____

_____

- →

· Amazing things I experienced today: ·

_____

_____

_____

· What am I looking forward to tomorrow? ·

_____

_____

_____

DATE:

○ · Today I am grateful for ·

_____

_____

_____

· What would make today great? ·

_____

_____

_____

· Positive affirmations. I am... ·

_____

_____

- →

☽ · Amazing things I experienced today: ·

_____

_____

_____

· What am I looking forward to tomorrow? ·

_____

_____

_____

DATE:

☀ · Today I am grateful for ·

_____

_____

_____

· What would make today great? ·

_____

_____

_____

· Positive affirmations. I am... ·

_____

_____

- →

☾ · Amazing things I experienced today: ·

_____

_____

_____

· What am I looking forward to tomorrow? ·

_____

_____

_____

· Today I am grateful for ·

_____

_____

_____

· What would make today great? ·

_____

_____

_____

· Positive affirmations. I am... ·

_____

_____

- →

· Amazing things I experienced today: ·

_____

_____

_____

· What am I looking forward to tomorrow? ·

_____

_____

_____

Patricia Watson
773-879-3700

Mind, Body, Wellness Retreat
Agenda

9-9:30 am Breakfast
9:30-10 am Welcome
10-11:30 am Mind
11:30-1 pm Lunch
1-2:30 pm Body & Wellness
2:30-3 pm Reflection

· Today I am grateful for ·

_____

_____

_____

· What would make today great? ·

_____

_____

_____

· Positive affirmations. I am... ·

_____

_____

- ➤

· Amazing things I experienced today: ·

_____

_____

_____

· What am I looking forward to tomorrow? ·

_____

_____

_____

· Today I am grateful for ·

_____

_____

_____

· What would make today great? ·

_____

_____

_____

· Positive affirmations. I am... ·

_____

_____

- →

· Amazing things I experienced today: ·

_____

_____

_____

· What am I looking forward to tomorrow? ·

_____

_____

_____

· Today I am grateful for ·

_____

_____

_____

· What would make today great? ·

_____

_____

_____

· Positive affirmations. I am... ·

_____

_____

_____

- ➤

· Amazing things I experienced today: ·

_____

_____

_____

· What am I looking forward to tomorrow? ·

_____

_____

_____

WEEKLY INSPIRATION

"

HAPPINESS IS A BALL AFTER WHICH WE
RUN WHEREVER IT ROLLS, AND WE PUSH IT
WITH OUR FEET WHEN IT STOPS.

"

—

Johann Wolfgang von Goethe

WRITE YOUR OWN QUOTE:

"

"

· Today I am grateful for ·

· What would make today great? ·

· Positive affirmations. I am... ·

· Amazing things I experienced today: ·

· What am I looking forward to tomorrow? ·

DATE:

☀ · Today I am grateful for ·

_____

_____

_____

· What would make today great? ·

_____

_____

_____

· Positive affirmations. I am... ·

_____

_____

✂- ➤

☾ · Amazing things I experienced today: ·

_____

_____

_____

· What am I looking forward to tomorrow? ·

_____

_____

_____

- Today I am grateful for -

_____

_____

_____

- What would make today great? -

_____

_____

_____

- Positive affirmations. I am... -

_____

_____

- ➤

- Amazing things I experienced today: -

_____

_____

_____

- What am I looking forward to tomorrow? -

_____

_____

_____

DATE:

☼ · Today I am grateful for ·

· What would make today great? ·

· Positive affirmations. I am... ·

✂ - →

☾ · Amazing things I experienced today: ·

· What am I looking forward to tomorrow? ·

44

· Today I am grateful for ·

_____

_____

_____

· What would make today great? ·

_____

_____

_____

· Positive affirmations. I am... ·

_____

_____

- ➤

· Amazing things I experienced today: ·

_____

_____

_____

· What am I looking forward to tomorrow? ·

_____

_____

_____

☼

· Today I am grateful for ·

_____

_____

_____

· What would make today great? ·

_____

_____

_____

· Positive affirmations. I am... ·

_____

_____

✂ - →

☽

· Amazing things I experienced today: ·

_____

_____

_____

· What am I looking forward to tomorrow? ·

_____

_____

_____

· Today I am grateful for ·

· What would make today great? ·

· Positive affirmations. I am... ·

· Amazing things I experienced today: ·

· What am I looking forward to tomorrow? ·

WEEKLY INSPIRATION

"

TO ACHIEVE GREATNESS ONE SHOULD LIVE AS IF THEY WILL NEVER DIE.

"

—

Francois de La Rochefoucauld

WRITE YOUR OWN QUOTE:

"

"

· Today I am grateful for ·

_____

_____

_____

· What would make today great? ·

_____

_____

_____

· Positive affirmations. I am... ·

_____

_____

_____

- →

· Amazing things I experienced today: ·

_____

_____

_____

· What am I looking forward to tomorrow? ·

_____

_____

_____

· Today I am grateful for ·

_____

_____

_____

· What would make today great? ·

_____

_____

_____

· Positive affirmations. I am... ·

_____

_____

- ➤

· Amazing things I experienced today: ·

_____

_____

_____

· What am I looking forward to tomorrow? ·

_____

_____

_____

· Today I am grateful for ·

_____

_____

_____

· What would make today great? ·

_____

_____

_____

· Positive affirmations. I am... ·

_____

_____

_____

- ➤

· Amazing things I experienced today: ·

_____

_____

_____

· What am I looking forward to tomorrow? ·

_____

_____

_____

DATE:

☀

· Today I am grateful for ·

_____

_____

_____

· What would make today great? ·

_____

_____

_____

· Positive affirmations. I am... ·

_____

_____

_____

- ➤

☾

· Amazing things I experienced today: ·

_____

_____

_____

· What am I looking forward to tomorrow? ·

_____

_____

_____

· Today I am grateful for ·

_____

_____

_____

· What would make today great? ·

_____

_____

_____

· Positive affirmations. I am... ·

_____

_____

- →

· Amazing things I experienced today: ·

_____

_____

_____

· What am I looking forward to tomorrow? ·

_____

_____

_____

DATE:

☀ · Today I am grateful for ·

_____

_____

_____

· What would make today great? ·

_____

_____

_____

· Positive affirmations. I am... ·

_____

_____

- ➤

☽ · Amazing things I experienced today: ·

_____

_____

_____

· What am I looking forward to tomorrow? ·

_____

_____

_____

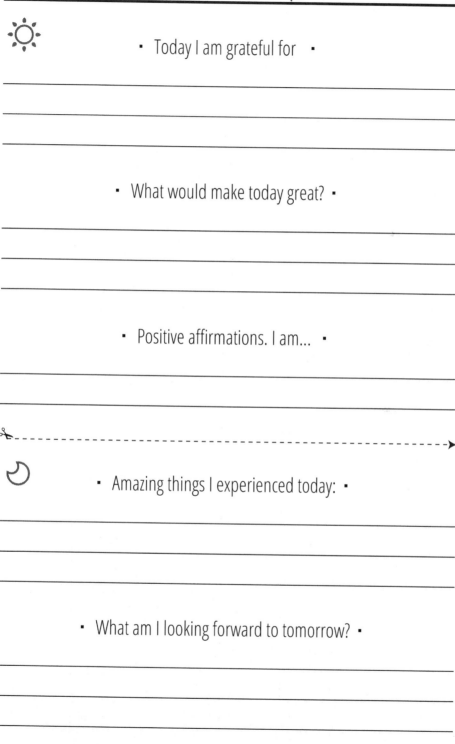

• Today I am grateful for •

• What would make today great? •

• Positive affirmations. I am... •

• Amazing things I experienced today: •

• What am I looking forward to tomorrow? •

WEEKLY INSPIRATION

"

GRATITUDE IS A DUTY WHICH OUGHT TO BE PAID, BUT WHICH NONE HAVE A RIGHT TO EXPECT.

"

–
Cicero

WRITE YOUR OWN QUOTE:

"

"

· Today I am grateful for ·

· What would make today great? ·

· Positive affirmations. I am... ·

· Amazing things I experienced today: ·

· What am I looking forward to tomorrow? ·

☼ · Today I am grateful for ·

_____

_____

_____

· What would make today great? ·

_____

_____

_____

· Positive affirmations. I am... ·

_____

_____

--->

☽ · Amazing things I experienced today: ·

_____

_____

_____

· What am I looking forward to tomorrow? ·

_____

_____

_____

· Today I am grateful for ·

_____

_____

_____

· What would make today great? ·

_____

_____

_____

· Positive affirmations. I am... ·

_____

_____

- →

· Amazing things I experienced today: ·

_____

_____

_____

· What am I looking forward to tomorrow? ·

_____

_____

_____

☼ · Today I am grateful for ·

_____

_____

· What would make today great? ·

_____

_____

· Positive affirmations. I am... ·

_____

_____

- →

☽ · Amazing things I experienced today: ·

_____

_____

· What am I looking forward to tomorrow? ·

_____

_____

_____

- Today I am grateful for ·

_____

_____

_____

· What would make today great? ·

_____

_____

_____

· Positive affirmations. I am... ·

_____

_____

- ➤

· Amazing things I experienced today: ·

_____

_____

_____

· What am I looking forward to tomorrow? ·

_____

_____

_____

· Today I am grateful for ·

_____

_____

_____

· What would make today great? ·

_____

_____

_____

· Positive affirmations. I am... ·

_____

_____

_____

- ➤

· Amazing things I experienced today: ·

_____

_____

_____

· What am I looking forward to tomorrow? ·

_____

_____

_____

_____

- Today I am grateful for -

_____

_____

_____

- What would make today great? -

_____

_____

_____

- Positive affirmations. I am... -

_____

_____

- Amazing things I experienced today: -

_____

_____

_____

- What am I looking forward to tomorrow? -

_____

_____

_____

WEEKLY INSPIRATION

" THE MOST BEAUTIFUL THINGS IN THE WORLD CANNOT BE SEEN OR EVEN TOUCHED, THEY MUST BE FELT WITH THE HEART. "

-

Helen Keller

WRITE YOUR OWN QUOTE:

"

"

· Today I am grateful for ·

· What would make today great? ·

· Positive affirmations. I am... ·

· Amazing things I experienced today: ·

· What am I looking forward to tomorrow? ·

☀

· Today I am grateful for ·

_____

_____

_____

· What would make today great? ·

_____

_____

_____

· Positive affirmations. I am... ·

_____

_____

_____

✂- →

☾

· Amazing things I experienced today: ·

_____

_____

_____

· What am I looking forward to tomorrow? ·

_____

_____

_____

_____

DATE:

· Today I am grateful for ·

_____

_____

_____

· What would make today great? ·

_____

_____

_____

· Positive affirmations. I am... ·

_____

_____

- ->

· Amazing things I experienced today: ·

_____

_____

_____

· What am I looking forward to tomorrow? ·

_____

_____

_____

☼ · Today I am grateful for ·

_____

_____

_____

· What would make today great? ·

_____

_____

_____

· Positive affirmations. I am... ·

_____

_____

_____

✂ - →

☾ · Amazing things I experienced today: ·

_____

_____

_____

· What am I looking forward to tomorrow? ·

_____

_____

_____

· Today I am grateful for ·

_____

_____

_____

· What would make today great? ·

_____

_____

_____

· Positive affirmations. I am... ·

_____

_____

- →

· Amazing things I experienced today: ·

_____

_____

_____

· What am I looking forward to tomorrow? ·

_____

_____

_____

· Today I am grateful for ·

_____

_____

_____

· What would make today great? ·

_____

_____

_____

· Positive affirmations. I am... ·

_____

_____

- ➤

· Amazing things I experienced today: ·

_____

_____

_____

· What am I looking forward to tomorrow? ·

_____

_____

_____

· Today I am grateful for ·

· What would make today great? ·

· Positive affirmations. I am... ·

· Amazing things I experienced today: ·

· What am I looking forward to tomorrow? ·

WEEKLY INSPIRATION

"

A LIFE SPENT MAKING MISTAKES IS NOT ONLY MORE HONORABLE, BUT MORE USEFUL THAN A LIFE SPENT DOING NOTHING.

"

–

George Bernard Shaw

WRITE YOUR OWN QUOTE:

"

"

DATE:

☼

· Today I am grateful for ·

_____

_____

_____

· What would make today great? ·

_____

_____

_____

· Positive affirmations. I am... ·

_____

_____

- →

☾

· Amazing things I experienced today: ·

_____

_____

_____

· What am I looking forward to tomorrow? ·

_____

_____

_____

☼

· Today I am grateful for ·

_____

_____

_____

· What would make today great? ·

_____

_____

_____

· Positive affirmations. I am... ·

_____

_____

_____

- ➤

☾

· Amazing things I experienced today: ·

_____

_____

_____

· What am I looking forward to tomorrow? ·

_____

_____

_____

· Today I am grateful for ·

· What would make today great? ·

· Positive affirmations. I am... ·

· Amazing things I experienced today: ·

· What am I looking forward to tomorrow? ·

· Today I am grateful for ·

· What would make today great? ·

· Positive affirmations. I am... ·

· Amazing things I experienced today: ·

· What am I looking forward to tomorrow? ·

· Today I am grateful for ·

· What would make today great? ·

· Positive affirmations. I am... ·

· Amazing things I experienced today: ·

· What am I looking forward to tomorrow? ·

· Today I am grateful for ·

_____

_____

_____

· What would make today great? ·

_____

_____

_____

· Positive affirmations. I am... ·

_____

_____

- →

· Amazing things I experienced today: ·

_____

_____

_____

· What am I looking forward to tomorrow? ·

_____

_____

_____

· Today I am grateful for ·

· What would make today great? ·

· Positive affirmations. I am... ·

· Amazing things I experienced today: ·

· What am I looking forward to tomorrow? ·

WEEKLY INSPIRATION

"

IT IS NOT DOING THE THING WE LIKE TO
DO, BUT LIKING THE THING WE HAVE TO
DO, THAT MAKES LIFE BLESSED.

"

–

Johann Wolfgang von Goethe

WRITE YOUR OWN QUOTE:

"

"

DATE:

☼

· Today I am grateful for ·

_____

_____

_____

· What would make today great? ·

_____

_____

_____

· Positive affirmations. I am... ·

_____

_____

✂ - ➤

☾

· Amazing things I experienced today: ·

_____

_____

_____

· What am I looking forward to tomorrow? ·

_____

_____

_____

☼

· Today I am grateful for ·

_____

_____

_____

· What would make today great? ·

_____

_____

_____

· Positive affirmations. I am... ·

_____

_____

_____

- ->

☾

· Amazing things I experienced today: ·

_____

_____

_____

· What am I looking forward to tomorrow? ·

_____

_____

_____

_____

· Today I am grateful for ·

· What would make today great? ·

· Positive affirmations. I am... ·

· Amazing things I experienced today: ·

· What am I looking forward to tomorrow? ·

☼ · Today I am grateful for ·

· What would make today great? ·

· Positive affirmations. I am... ·

✂ - →

☾ · Amazing things I experienced today: ·

· What am I looking forward to tomorrow? ·

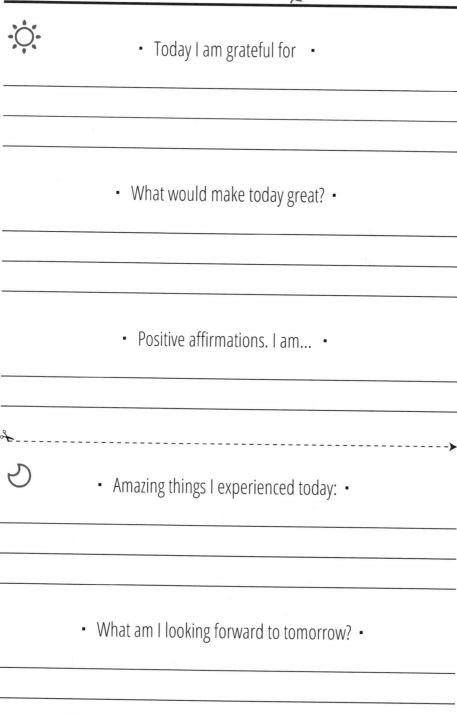

DATE:

· Today I am grateful for ·

_____

_____

_____

· What would make today great? ·

_____

_____

_____

· Positive affirmations. I am... ·

_____

_____

- ➤

· Amazing things I experienced today: ·

_____

_____

_____

· What am I looking forward to tomorrow? ·

_____

_____

_____

- Today I am grateful for -

_____

_____

_____

- What would make today great? -

_____

_____

_____

- Positive affirmations. I am... -

_____

_____

- ➤

- Amazing things I experienced today: -

_____

_____

_____

- What am I looking forward to tomorrow? -

_____

_____

_____

· Today I am grateful for ·

· What would make today great? ·

· Positive affirmations. I am... ·

· Amazing things I experienced today: ·

· What am I looking forward to tomorrow? ·

WEEKLY INSPIRATION

"

TO ACCOMPLISH GREAT THINGS, WE MUST
NOT ONLY ACT, BUT ALSO DREAM; NOT
ONLY PLAN, BUT ALSO BELIEVE.

"

–

Anatole France

WRITE YOUR OWN QUOTE:

"

"

• Today I am grateful for •

• What would make today great? •

• Positive affirmations. I am... •

- →

• Amazing things I experienced today: •

• What am I looking forward to tomorrow? •

· Today I am grateful for ·

· What would make today great? ·

· Positive affirmations. I am... ·

- →

· Amazing things I experienced today: ·

· What am I looking forward to tomorrow? ·

DATE:

☼

· Today I am grateful for ·

_____

_____

_____

· What would make today great? ·

_____

_____

_____

· Positive affirmations. I am... ·

_____

_____

- ➤

🌙

· Amazing things I experienced today: ·

_____

_____

_____

· What am I looking forward to tomorrow? ·

_____

_____

_____

☀ · Today I am grateful for ·

_____

_____

_____

· What would make today great? ·

_____

_____

_____

· Positive affirmations. I am... ·

_____

_____

- ➤

☾ · Amazing things I experienced today: ·

_____

_____

_____

· What am I looking forward to tomorrow? ·

_____

_____

_____

- Today I am grateful for -

_____

_____

_____

- What would make today great? -

_____

_____

_____

- Positive affirmations. I am... -

_____

_____

- ➤

- Amazing things I experienced today: -

_____

_____

_____

- What am I looking forward to tomorrow? -

_____

_____

_____

DATE:

☀

· Today I am grateful for ·

_____

_____

_____

· What would make today great? ·

_____

_____

_____

· Positive affirmations. I am... ·

_____

_____

_____

✂ - ➤

☾

· Amazing things I experienced today: ·

_____

_____

_____

· What am I looking forward to tomorrow? ·

_____

_____

_____

· Today I am grateful for ·

_____

_____

_____

· What would make today great? ·

_____

_____

_____

· Positive affirmations. I am... ·

_____

_____

- ➤

· Amazing things I experienced today: ·

_____

_____

_____

· What am I looking forward to tomorrow? ·

_____

_____

_____

WEEKLY INSPIRATION

"

EVERYTHING HAS BEAUTY, BUT NOT EVERYONE SEES IT.

"

—

Confucius

WRITE YOUR OWN QUOTE:

"

"

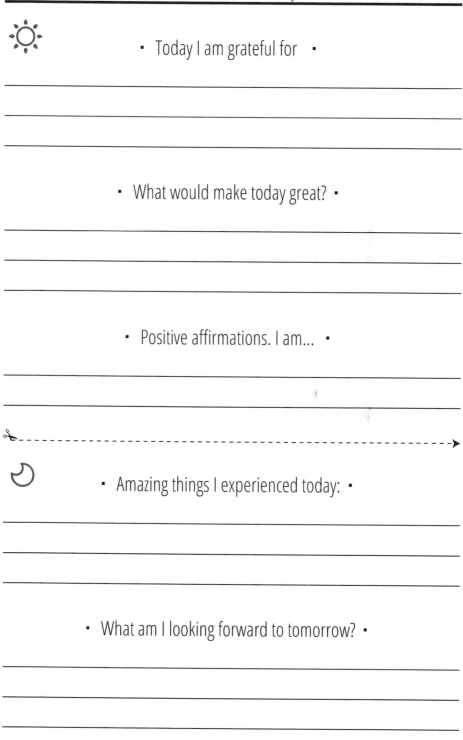

DATE:

· Today I am grateful for ·

· What would make today great? ·

· Positive affirmations. I am... ·

· Amazing things I experienced today: ·

· What am I looking forward to tomorrow? ·

DATE:

☀ · Today I am grateful for ·

_____

_____

_____

· What would make today great? ·

_____

_____

_____

· Positive affirmations. I am... ·

_____

_____

_____

✂ --➤

🌙 · Amazing things I experienced today: ·

_____

_____

_____

· What am I looking forward to tomorrow? ·

_____

_____

_____

☀

· Today I am grateful for ·

_____

_____

_____

· What would make today great? ·

_____

_____

_____

· Positive affirmations. I am... ·

_____

_____

✂ - →

☾

· Amazing things I experienced today: ·

_____

_____

_____

· What am I looking forward to tomorrow? ·

_____

_____

_____

☀

· Today I am grateful for ·

_____

_____

· What would make today great? ·

_____

_____

· Positive affirmations. I am... ·

_____

_____

✂ - ➤

☾

· Amazing things I experienced today: ·

_____

_____

· What am I looking forward to tomorrow? ·

_____

_____

_____

· Today I am grateful for ·

_____

_____

_____

· What would make today great? ·

_____

_____

_____

· Positive affirmations. I am... ·

_____

_____

- →

· Amazing things I experienced today: ·

_____

_____

_____

· What am I looking forward to tomorrow? ·

_____

_____

_____

DATE:

☀

· Today I am grateful for ·

_____

_____

_____

· What would make today great? ·

_____

_____

_____

· Positive affirmations. I am... ·

_____

_____

_____

☾

· Amazing things I experienced today: ·

_____

_____

_____

· What am I looking forward to tomorrow? ·

_____

_____

_____

· Today I am grateful for ·

_____

_____

_____

· What would make today great? ·

_____

_____

_____

· Positive affirmations. I am... ·

_____

_____

_____

- ➤

· Amazing things I experienced today: ·

_____

_____

_____

· What am I looking forward to tomorrow? ·

_____

_____

_____

WEEKLY INSPIRATION

" WHEN A PERSON REALLY DESIRES
SOMETHING, ALL THE UNIVERSE CONSPIRES
TO HELP THAT PERSON TO REALIZE HIS
DREAM. **"**

–

Lucy Larcom

WRITE YOUR OWN QUOTE:

"

"

Made in the USA
San Bernardino, CA
20 March 2019